IT'S
ABOUT
THE STUDENTS

Devotions
FOR
Teachers

EDWARD C. GRUBE

CONCORDIA PUBLISHING HOUSE · SAINT LOUIS

Written by Edward C. Grube

Edited by Rodney L. Rathmann

This publication may be available in braille, in large print, or on cassette tape
for the visually impaired. Please allow 8 to 12 weeks for delivery. Write to
Lutheran Blind Mission, 7550 Watson Rd., St. Louis, MO 63119-4409; call
toll-free 1-888-215-2455; or visit the Web site: www.blindmission.org.

1 2 3 4 5 6 7 8 9 10   20 19 18 17 16 15 14 13 12 11

Devotions

 This book is for **Logan**,

whose blessings may not seem as apparent as those in children born with perfect chromosomes, but whose faith flourishes— as will the rest of his life—in praise to a loving God and gratitude to Christian parents and his sister, as well as thanks for the faith-based support of his extended family of Lutheran educators.

FOREWORD

The Kids in Your Class

Imagine a classroom filled with forty students, all of whom are characters in the Bible. Of course, it would be nice if all the students were like Ruth or Jesus, but that wouldn't be fair. Or real. You'll always have your impetuous Peters, self-promoting Judases, or bullying Jezebels. You'll find these and more on the pages of this devotional book.

But this isn't just about the students. It's about the Master Teacher. And it's about you, the teacher who is also a student of the Master. God has left us a legacy of learning. May God grant you the ability to learn from Jesus, from biblical characters, and from your students.

The devotions presume background knowledge of the "students." Many are well-known. Some might make you want to read more about them to get a better understanding of their role in God's history of salvation. Extended Bible reading suggestions appear at the end of each meditation.

Sketches of the "students" claim no historical accuracy. They are the writer's imagination based on historical background. Any resemblance to real students in your classroom is purely coincidental. And highly probable.

Edward Grube
SPRING 2011

1

Adam

. . . .

When no bush of the field was yet in the land and no small plant of the field had yet sprung up—for the LORD God had not caused it to rain on the land, and there was no man to work the ground, and a mist was going up from the land and was watering the whole face of the ground— then the LORD God formed the man of dust from the ground and breathed into his nostrils the breath of life, and the man became a living creature. (Genesis 2:5–7)

. . . .

Imagine that Adam is in your class. Is anyone more eager? He is the first to arrive every day, and he takes special delight in feeding the fish, calling each by name as they rise to the fish flakes or dart toward the sinking food. The classroom gerbil gets a pat, and Adam even hums a little tune to the snake, which he handles without fear. Then it's off to water the plants, checking on the progress of the beans and marigolds. If he has any fault, it's that he always seems a bit dusty and takes special pride in the dirt under his finger-nails. Adam worked pretty much by himself until a new girl enrolled. She has an irresistible smile and a mind of her own. They developed a major crush on each other. They like to share their snacks.

Wouldn't it have been exciting to teach at Paradise Lutheran School? Garden recesses and choir practices would decorate the days. Not that your days go without adornment. You have good ones—or at least good parts of days. What are some of your best teaching memories? Take a few minutes right now to thank God for them.

No day is ideal. Sin sullies the classroom and everyone in it. You have vivid memories of those moments too. Maybe you even caused some of them! Take a few more moments right now to ac-knowledge your guilt—and thank Jesus for taking away your sins.

That wasn't hard, was it? That's because God did all the work through the life, death, and resurrection of Jesus! You are a forgiven sinner. Not only is that reason for celebration (and relief!) but it's also the source of power to pay forward what you have received. Your class may not be a Garden of Eden, but because you teach and pray according to His Word, it is a place where God dwells in all of His mercy and grace.

Though it may be in your dreams, you're not ready yet for perfect days. You must cultivate the gifts God provided, tarnished and fragile and choked by weeds as they may be at times. Each child in your class is a life that God has enrolled in your care. And for some of those kids, you care more than anyone else on earth. God has made you a gift to them. You are gifts to one another, gifts that share the first gift ever given!

❖ **Background Reading:**
Genesis 1:26–31

2

Peter

∙ ∙ ∙ ∙ ∙ ∙ ∙ ∙ ∙ ∙ ∙ ∙ ∙ ∙ ∙

If then God gave the same gift to them as He gave to us when we believed the Lord Jesus Christ, who was I that I could stand in God's way? (Acts 11:17)

∙ ∙ ∙ ∙ ∙ ∙ ∙ ∙ ∙ ∙ ∙ ∙ ∙ ∙ ∙

Imagine that Peter is in your class. He is a good kid that you can trust, though you harbor a few reservations when he is in one of his impetuous moods. He could sit in the back row and be an asset to the other students and you. But he chooses the front row, where he can see, hear, and contribute sans a sea of bobbing heads to impede progress. Peter's only fault is his unswerving allegiance to rules. (Fault you say? Would that all students suffered such malaise!) Lunch provides an illustrative example. School rules require nutritious meals. Peter checks the ingredients against the standards. He would rather go hungry than ingest a few extra grains of sugar or salt.

So what does the Christian teacher learn from Peter? You learn to grow and to adjust to change.

Peter's life is recorded in the Gospels and in the Acts of the Apostles, which expose Peter's bravado of allegiance to Jesus that melts into sorrow, shame, and deep humility. You find a man gone from rags to riches—the rags of a Jewish fisherman's orthodox conformity to the riches of freedom and fresh life through faith in the Savior. Peter would attest that it isn't an easy transformation.

Teachers must grow, and there are many ways to do it. Each requires an individualized education plan. What is yours? First for everyone must be repentance. You are mature enough to admit your sins, so that's not a problem. The work of resisting future temptation may be more difficult, and sometimes you settle for simply hating your sins.

Growth continues, its potential fueled by repentance and forgiveness. How do you use Law and Gospel in your teaching? As freeing as the Gospel is, you might paradoxically prefer the Law at times. Teaching legitimately involves demands, discipline, and doing. Success, no matter how small (or delusionary), feeds the desire to accomplish more, more, and even more. Then failure plunders the process. Only the sweet salvation of the Gospel, freely given, provides relief, comfort, and the confession that only Jesus saves, and He did it for you.

The Law, and all its attending rules, is for people. God made it for the good of those He loves. But Peter became confused at first about God's Law. He subscribed to the school of thought that demanded obedience for salvation—no matter that salvation was already accomplished!

Peter grew as God led him to know that the devout Jewish diet put Jesus in a box. No dining habit could stand between potential believers and their Savior. It had to be a struggle for such an obedient teacher to adjust—to eat the unbelievers' food so as not to offend them and slam the door to faith.

Your salvation is sure. You know the truth and the comfort of salvation. It may take a while for some of your students to do things like go to church, remember to pray, and read the Bible. It may even take fifty or sixty years! No need to fret. Just don't limit the possibilities of how God works. Look at what He did for you!

❖ **Background reading:**
   Acts 11:1–18

3

Jonah

. . . .

I went down to the land whose bars closed upon me forever; yet You brought up my life from the pit, O LORD my God. When my life was fainting away, I remembered the LORD, and my prayer came to You, into Your holy temple.
(Jonah 2:6–7)

. . . .

Imagine that Jonah is in your class. He is the one with great potential—if only he could refocus his ingenuity toward accomplishing objectives rather than getting out of assignments.

Most people have a little Jonah in them—even dedicated teachers like you. Some days, you are intimidated by the classroom—or a belligerent board or predatory parents gathering for their afternoon hunt. If it's not intimidation, then it might be the enormity of the task. No matter what you do, some students just don't respond. Perhaps it's better to do something else; after all, replacing classroom stress with a modest savings account might offer an enjoyable alternative.

Please don't leave.

You have much to offer, and all of it is in the name of Jesus, by the call of God, and by the power of the Holy Spirit.

You probably won't see your students wandering in sackcloth and covered with ashes—unless someone forgot to lock the furnace-room door. In fact, you're not likely to witness results anything like the dramatic reaction of Jonah's call to repentance. (On the plus side, your kids probably aren't as bad as the Ninevites.) Remember, success isn't your responsibility. The Holy Spirit takes full responsibility.

The strangest twist in Jonah's highly unusual story is his reaction to success, mercy, and grace. He appeared not to like any of them. Is there anything that would cause you to react that way? Could grace be a problem?

God lavishes His grace on all. He is equally merciful to all who sin. So, the parent who rattles your eardrum and attacks your character is as forgiven as you, who so patiently (ahem) absorbs the abuse. And so the question, which you probably avoid vocalizing, is something like, "How fair is this? If only God would give people what they deserve . . .?"

It took only one sin to require the cross. And you didn't even commit it! But then, you claim enough of your own. Because you teach in a Christian school, you might face temptation to be smug or a bit self-righteous. You are, after all, making sacrifices to do what you're doing where you're doing it. Don't you deserve better?

You know the answer. You know it without going overboard. Someday maybe you and Jonah will chat about it. You deserve death, but God, through Jesus Christ, has saved you. When you're in a spiritual or emotional pit, do what Jonah did. Cry to God for help. When you're "fainting away" with fatigue or fear, follow Jonah's example. God will strengthen you. If you find yourself heading away from your work rather than facing it straight on, ask the Holy Spirit to spin you around and send you where He wants you to go.

And it might be good to stay away from boats.

❖ **Background Reading:**

Jonah 1

4

Elisha

. . . .

When the servant of the man of God rose early in the morning and went out, behold, an army with horses and chariots was all around the city. And the servant said, "Alas, my master! What shall we do?" He said, "Do not be afraid, for those who are with us are more than those who are with them." Then Elisha prayed and said, "O LORD, please open his eyes that he may see." So the LORD opened the eyes of the young man, and he saw, and behold, the mountain was full of horses and chariots of fire all around Elisha. (2 Kings 6:15–17)

. . . .

Imagine that Elisha is in your class. He is a sensitive young boy with a tendency of making right of wrong. He is the best bully fighter in the whole school. In fact, the diminishing number of bullies gives testimony to his effectiveness. Elisha doesn't tolerate anyone speaking against the one true God. Kids who swear do it only once in front of Elisha. They are no match for his retribution. But any friend of God finds a true friend in Elisha.

You need to be an Elisha for your children.

You know there is a battle going on for their souls. Satan's army would appear to have the upper hand. You can identify some of the dangers in media temptations and influence. Violent disregard for life, sick sensuality, self-centered humanism, and disintegrating spiritual values are easily identifiable. Add behind-the-scenes battles waged by demons, and the jeopardy seems impossible to escape or resist. Some things haven't changed over the centuries since Elisha's ministry.

God's forces outnumber the devil's forces. As if God even needed warrior angels! As Martin Luther said, "One little word can fell him [Satan]."

Children may be terrified to think of the battles fought outside their perception. But they will be comforted to know that Jesus fought to win them. And you. The battle raged on the ground as Jesus, true man, fought a barrage of temptations to live a life of perfection on behalf of you and your students. The battle raged in the air as Jesus hung on the cross, sacrificing His life to pay for our sins. And the victory was won underground, in the tomb, as Jesus defeated death and the devil once and for all times. This is the war that students need to know. This is the war that you must memorialize.

The war is won, but the defeated enemy will not surrender. Pray for your students. And if they sometimes think they are alone or outnumbered in their young Christian lives, read to them. Help them see what Elisha saw—a powerful army protects them.

❖ **Background Reading:**

2 Kings 2:15–22

5

Paul

. . . .

For I do not do the good I want, but the evil I do not want is what I keep on doing. (Romans 7:19)

. . . .

Imagine that Paul is in your class. Were votes cast, he would win the title for "most changed student." He would go from driven to . . . to . . . to, well, still driven. The biggest change is in whose name he now finds his drive. While his original drive was motivated by Satan, his new zeal is in the name of Jesus and aimed at enemies of Jesus. He can be diplomatic or he can be terse; either way, he makes his message clear. Yet he often argues in circles, mostly with himself. His sentence structure is the stuff of disciplinary sentence diagramming!

Some teachers want to be like the apostle Paul. How about you? The travel and the rapt crowds might be attractive—an itinerant teacher. Of course, many of Paul's travels included beatings and jail time. But Paul regarded all his experiences worth the sacrifice. He knew that Jesus' sacrifice was greater. He just had to tell others about the Savior.

Your missionary journeys take you to the classroom and to other nearby locations. Sure beats sailing surging seas and walking the soles off your sandals! No drive through clogged construction zones exceeds Paul's experience! Your missionary journey takes you to the fertile mission field called your classroom. (A great place to visit even if you wouldn't want to live there. Though maybe you do [live there].)

You can't assume that you know specific mission targets on your seating chart. Many of your students confess belief in Jesus as their Savior, and it's not your mission to question the faith of others. Some children may seem obvious candidates—no spiritual life, not baptized, ignorant of Scripture. They may need your special care—your gentle word and the role you not only model but also live. And yes, you may take some verbal or emotional beatings as you minister to such students. Paul would count such treatment a privilege of service.

Paul's missionary status was indeed a special status conferred on him. He couldn't figure out that one! He knew what he had been—how he contributed to the persecution of believers. Beyond that, Paul experienced the same struggle you do. He knew the tenets of Christian life, but sin stubbornly tried to drag him in opposite directions. Do you contend with sinful nature too? That may be an asset for missionaries, modern and ancient alike.

The more you struggle and suffer with sin's power, the more wonderful and welcome the Gospel message is! If you are cured from cancer, your gratitude will be much greater than if you were saved from a splinter. And your testimony will be all the more powerful.

Sinners relate to one another. So you and your students have much in common. Many sins. Complete forgiveness. Those who already know Jesus will never tire of that message. Those who don't know Him will find such love hard to believe.

The Holy Spirit will take care of that problem.

❖ **Background reading:**
Acts 9:1–19

6

Jezebel

· · · · · · · · · · · · · · · ·

And as if it had been a light thing for him to walk in the sins of Jeroboam the son of Nebat, he took for his wife Jezebel the daughter of Ethbaal king of the Sidonians, and went and served Baal and worshiped him. (1 Kings 16:31)

· · · · · · · · · · · · · · · ·

Imagine that Jezebel is in your class. (Now if that doesn't raise goose bumps, you are an exceptionally calm person.) Jezebel is the meanest girl in the class. In fact, she is the meanest anything anywhere! She is the sort to bully and badger other girls until she drives them to desperation. She has her ways with the boys. They will do anything for her—the more terrible the task, the greater the reward. She has left a long trail of broken spirits and an army of malicious rebels behind. Jezebel is queen of crude, shrewd, and lewd.

So why does the school tolerate her? She has powerful friends. You will not succeed in transforming her life. She will probably die young, a victim of her own lifestyle. She won't be among the students with whom you'll have a joyful reunion in heaven.

The real Jezebel witnessed dramatic demonstrations of God's power. Despite those blasts of the Law, which usually cost others their lives, Jezebel refused to repent. And if she had? She would have witnessed an even more powerful blast of God's grace. It wasn't for lack of God's attention that Jezebel failed. It was her own evil will and unyielding heart.

Teaching is all about success. You are held accountable for kids who don't learn according to their ability. That's what is so frustrating about teaching. And it is downright tormenting in Christian schools! Students must not only learn Scripture and faith from you but also believe it. You so badly want them to believe it! But it's not up to you. Success is by the power of the Holy Spirit, and rejecting the Good News is not cause for blaming you.

None of this lets you off the hook. Even if you're 99.9 percent sure that a Jezebel occupies (part-time anyway) seat 5 in row 4, you must continue teaching the Law and offering the Gospel. Now, now, no moaning or debating allowed. Remember Jonah?

One joy of teaching in a Christian school is the emphasis on never surrendering a child. God has placed in your mind-set a little reminder that Jesus died for all children and that He wants every single one to come to faith in Him. He also tempers that mind-set with knowledge that not all who hear His Word will believe it. You don't have to waste energy on judging your success. Spend that energy praying instead. Pray that someday all the power that the Holy Spirit poured out on behalf of this or that child will bear fruit. The lesson, of course, is to persist with courage. Don't let your Jezebel frighten you, even if she has parents and other students who support and fuel her wickedness. Pray for her. Love her. Maybe even keep her away from open windows (2 Kings 9:30–33).

> ❖ **Background Reading:**
> **1 Kings 21:1–16**

7

Habakkuk

· · · · · · · · · · · · · · · ·

Though the fig tree should not blossom, nor fruit be on the vines, the produce of the olive fail and the fields yield no food, the flock be cut off from the fold and there be no herd in the stalls, yet I will rejoice in the LORD; I will take joy in the God of my salvation. GOD, the Lord, is my strength. (Habakkuk 3:17–19a)

· · · · · · · · · · · · · · · ·

Imagine that Habakkuk is in your class. The most difficult thing about Habakkuk is spelling his name. It's even worse than Connecticut! Habakkuk is the class comforter. His optimism isn't quite contagious, but it does disrupt mutant conversations that lead to perpetual pity parties. He is the only one who sees a bright side to weather-cancelled recesses, mass failure on the geography test, and cancellation of the field trip. Habakkuk is able to place those minor inconveniences into perspective. And even in the worst of occasions, Habakkuk launches an animated show and tell—about how God cares for His people. If only Habakkuk's parents had christened him Herb!

Do you allow students to comfort you? Yes, it's a switch in roles, but humbly accepting a child's compassion is a gift both for the child and for you. Kids won't comfort you unless they know you need it. Now, now, don't subject your students to recurring mornings of mourning. But when you're hurting, let it show. Children need practice giving comfort gracefully. Teachers need practice accepting it graciously.

Though children seem to have a natural capacity for compassion, they must learn the true source of comfort and encouragement. That task falls to you.

When were you most in need of comfort? Perhaps it was as serious as a spouse diagnosed with a deadly disease or a phone call from the police at 3:00 a.m. Maybe it was less profound, like getting a tooth pulled or the death of a beloved pet. Okay, so the pet thing can be profound too. The only lasting source of comfort comes from God Himself. The more you learn about His comfort, the more you experience it yourself from His written and spoken Word, and the better you will be at modeling it for your kids to copy.

Sin is the cause for all need of comfort. Sometimes that sin comes from the outside; sometimes it is self-inflicted. The initial source of comfort starts with repentance and acknowledgement that God would never harm us. Next, we have the long, recorded history of comfort, ranging from messianic promise to Adam and Eve in Genesis to the vision of heaven in Revelation.

The cross of Christ is the cause for all comfort. The child's simple "Jesus loves me this I know . . ." is good for storms, sicknesses, and even death.

But back to the kids and you. Your school year is like the familiar drama masks, but it doesn't involve scripts and blocking. Real life in your classroom just happens, both joy and tragedy. May the Holy Spirit infuse your classroom with hope and the kind of optimism that has its roots in the history of salvation.

As for Habakkuk? Be thankful. He could be Stanislaus Herrkkamum from Azerbaijan.

> ❖ **Background Reading:**
> **Habakkuk 1:1–11**

8

Samuel

. . . .

*And the L*ORD *came and stood, calling as at other times, "Samuel! Samuel!" And Samuel said, "Speak, for Your servant hears." (1 Samuel 3:10)*

. . . .

Imagine that Samuel is in your class. (His mother said she would like to leave him there 24/7, but that's probably against the law.) He is the one whose name you have to call three times before he realizes you are talking to him. Normally, this isn't a problem, except in situations like the time you asked him to close the windows after class (and before the storm). Other than that, Samuel has the sometimes annoying asset of doing what is best and right, even when you are unsure. You fully expect that Samuel will one day direct powerful people. Or maybe become a pastor.

You are dedicated to teaching in a Christian school. No matter how you got that way—dedicated, that is—you don't share the experience of Samuel, and you're probably glad that you don't.

To be pledged into service before birth and sent to live away from home at an early age seems a little too intense. Yet your role in your school is neither accident nor coincidence.

Long before you were born, long before ancient Samuel was born, God knew you. He sent His Son to save you, and He sent you His Holy Spirit in Baptism. The Spirit guided you to where you are today. Not that where you serve is a bed of begonias. Satan and sin disturb and distract those who teach in the name of Jesus. The obstacles can be severe and disheartening. Satan would like you to get up and go when the going gets tough.

Frustration and dissuasion take other sin-scarred forms too. Your tough, right decisions may be unpopular or even overruled by those "in charge." Laboring in Jesus' name doesn't spare you opposition, but that opposition isn't as powerful as the One on whose side you minister.

What opposition confronts you as you teach in the name of Creator God and Savior Jesus? Is the Holy Spirit just a bunch of wind to some students and teachers?

Science may be one of those oppositional areas for which you need Samuel's resistance, insistence, and persistence. You cannot accept anti-biblical teaching just because it's shouted in your direction three, forty, or even fifty thousand times by experts in the field. Let those in error repeat their lie, deception, or confusion, but hear and teach what God wants to tell you in Scripture.

Other subjects easily propose similar threats. Literature valued for its profanity or anti-Christian themes may occupy prominent roles among colleagues who want to "broaden" students' perspectives. Some history resources use pseudo scholarship to skew facts. And then there is the psychosocial philosophy that makes self-governing gods of all people.

All this is preaching to the choir, isn't it? After all, you are a forgiven sinner teaching in a Christian school that is insulated from the world and its disrespect and mockery of God.

Get real, right?

Yes, you are a forgiven sinner. Beyond that, Christian schools are laboratories for learning, and sometimes your test tubes boil over. You need to know when to be tough and when to be gentle, and you must always be forthright. That's what will make you a teacher in the shadows not only of Samuel but also of the Master Teacher Himself.

❖ **Background reading:**
1 Samuel 1:1–20

9

John

. . . .

And I heard a loud voice from the throne saying, "Behold, the dwelling place of God is with man. He will dwell with them, and they will be His people, and God Himself will be with them as their God. He will wipe away every tear from their eyes, and death shall be no more, neither shall there be mourning, nor crying, nor pain anymore, for the former things have passed away." (Revelation 21:3–4)

. . . .

Imagine that John is in your classroom. (Common name. You have several. Some are a whole lot alike!) John is calm and dependable—a compassionate boy to whom you could entrust your mother, if circumstances required. John also is a visionary, not that he lacks a grasp of present reality. John is the intelligent observer. He listens and obeys and possesses a mature-for-his-age confidence in the future. He never worries about what he will be; he seems to know what his future holds.

While Jesus' other disciples met with violent ends, John lived through many perils. Perhaps his exile actually sheltered him from some dangers. Even during a time that would have many people wallowing in self-pity, despair, and depression, John was able to think of others and share a wonderful gift. Confined on an island, with little else to do, John could focus without distraction on what God wanted him to see and then report to God's people in far-off centuries.

When you were a student, did your graduating class inflict a tradition of class prophecies on one another? Those were intentional attempts to entertain the audience and influence their thoughts. If that happened to you, how did it turn out?

Teachers can't help but dream of their students' futures. Usually, they are only accidentally accurate. To be honest, sometimes they are tinged with a bit of malice toward uncooperative students. Yes, lapsing into fringes of fateful prophecy exacts revenge for the suffering some students have caused. That, as you know, is sin's way of dealing with the sins of others. Perhaps even the disciple John harbored ill visions of what should happen to the arrogant soldiers who executed his beloved Friend.

Repentance clears out the muck. You are forgiven to go on livin' with godly vision! Now, you are a visionary. Your visions aren't direct revelations from God, but they serve a godly purpose nonetheless. What do you see of your future and the futures of your students?

Do you see heaven, as John did? Look hard, now. You can do it. Whom do you see there? Family? Childhood friends—even a few you might not have regarded as friends? And there, off in the distance (aren't you surprised at what you can see in eternity?), aren't those the students whom you taught to sing "Jesus Loves Me, This I Know"? And—praise God!—isn't that your one student who got the death penalty for a life of crime? Jesus smiles and says something about a "deathbed" conversion and how He has seen a few of those!

Right now, thinking of spending eternity with a few of your students may not exactly seem like heaven. But admit it, you want to be there with all the students you ever served. Your vision will be blessed with divine reality.

❖ **Background Reading:**
Revelation 1:1–19

Sarah

· · · · · · · · · · · · · · · ·

And Sarah said, "God has made laughter for me; everyone who hears will laugh over me." (Genesis 21:6)

· · · · · · · · · · · · · · · ·

Imagine that Sarah is in your class. (Sometimes she writes her name *Sarai*, as it seems tp be the fashion for some adolescent girls to modify their names.) Sarah will probably be homecoming queen. She is beautiful, smart, and caring, and she giggles a lot. She giggles a whole lot when Abraham is nearby. Sarah is serious about her future. She would like to have a big family and enough money to afford it. Way in the back of her mind, though, she has this sinking feeling that a large family is an impossible dream. Yet, if she talks to God about it, maybe He will make her dream come true. She wonders if Abraham would make a good dad. He certainly doesn't stand around in one place very long!

Biblical Sarah's strength is her faith that God always will do His best for her. He has made some grand promises, which seem farther from reality with every year that she ages. She takes things into her own hands when she thinks God is waiting for her help to fulfill His promise. She helps Abraham get a son, but it's not hers, and it wasn't God's plan to make it happen this way. God's promise of a child once made her laugh, and it wasn't in glee. A gentle divine reprimand brought her back to the promise she so wanted to believe.

Have you ever giggled at God? Do you ever pray the impossible, smiling wryly at the near unfeasibility of fulfillment? Teachers pray for lots of impossibilities: all students earning straight-A report cards, parents who love their children enough to encourage them, a congregation so in love with its school that it won't allow impediments to its continuing operation. . . . What is your prayer?

What causes the doubtful giggle at God? Who has experienced the impossible? Searching for dramatic answers is unproductive. But wait. Hasn't the impossible already happened? Jesus died for all. And now, Jesus lives! Talk about incredible! God fulfilled His promise not for brainy students, conscientious families, or gung-ho congregations, but for the best miracle of all: eternal life in the presence of God.

Have you ever giggled with God? Now is the time. Release a big and long one. Probably shouldn't do this on a crowded elevator—but then again, why not? Laugh for yourself. Laugh for your students. You live in the joy of Jesus, and it's so important to show it. Some students aren't so sure about this Jesus thing. They have no acquaintance with His love—or maybe with anybody's love, for that matter. So let your classroom be happy and loving.

Yes, moral behavior—good discipline—is a benchmark of Christian schools. However, depending on good behavior to prove your Christian character will eventually fail you. Let your classroom be a place of forgiveness. Maybe the dismissal benediction should end with a giggle instead of an "amen."

❖ **Background Reading:**
Genesis 12:10–20

11

John
the Baptist

· · · · · · · · · · · · · · · ·

[John] said, "I am the voice of one crying out in the wilderness, 'Make straight the way of the Lord.'" (John 1:23)

· · · · · · · · · · · · · · · ·

Imagine that John the Baptist is in your class. He is the star of outdoor education, with an affinity for life in wilderness areas. His frequent absences are reluctantly welcome; he brings really weird snacks. Yet, as strange as John can be, classmates are oddly attracted to him. He spends recess standing on a milk crate, lecturing on preparedness to meet and greet some special stranger. You believe that John the Baptist's brutal honesty might someday lead to brutality against him.

Have you ever imagined yourself a John the Baptist-type teacher? Calling the class in from the playground doesn't count as a voice crying in the wilderness, but you may share other qualities. Let's try a personality inventory.

1. Do you tell others about Jesus, the Savior? Okay, that's a good start. Your Baptism qualifies you to proclaim the Gospel. Your training in Scripture is important too. Good teachers master content. John the Baptist was present when New Testament Scripture was conceived, so he was an eyewitness to God's testimony about Jesus. You get your content from hearing and reading God's Word. Continuing education is essential.

2. Are you spiritually courageous? It's easy to answer "yes," because you don't have a headhunter hot on your trail. John the Baptist had nothing but contempt for those who refused to believe that the Jesus he introduced was the Christ. He called self-serving unbelievers vipers, and no, herpetology wasn't a hobby. He flatly called sin, *sin*. John hoped that his honesty would lead to repentance. It did; but it also led to prison and execution. Would you sacrifice your life to tell the truth about Jesus? Pray that you will never face that test. But, emboldened by the Holy Spirit and assured of eternal life, you could be so brave.

3. Do you urge students to prepare for Jesus' second coming? This assumes that you yourself are prepared! A preparation checklist might include teaching and testing students on their knowledge of what God did for them through Jesus Christ. Old Testament Bible stories and catechesis might appear on the list. Regular worship and home devotions could be important. And don't forget prayer.

Ahem—there is this one thing about brutal honesty.

The truth is that nothing you or students do actually prepares you or them to meet Jesus. Jesus did it all. Did He live a perfect life? Check. Did He sacrifice His life to pay the penalty actually owed by sinners? Check. Did He defeat death and the power of the devil? BIG CHECK! If you and your students believe all that, then you are prepared. All the other things that we sometimes identify as *preparation* are things we want to do because of what Jesus did!

❖ **Background Reading:**
Luke 3:1–20

Miriam

· · · · · · · · · · · · · · ·

Then Miriam the prophetess, the sister of Aaron, took a tambourine in her hand, and all the women went out after her with tambourines and dancing. And Miriam sang to them: "Sing to the Lord, for He has triumphed gloriously; the horse and his rider He has thrown into the sea." *(Exodus 15:20–21)*

· · · · · · · · · · · · · · ·

Imagine that Miriam is in your class. She is the spontaneous, energetic, praise-band promoter. Her voice and backup percussion are enough to inspire toe-tapping praise during chapel. You expect dancing to break out any moment as others catch her musical ecstasy. Some classmates hope this kind of thing will happen all the time in heaven! Hmm. Better keep an eye on Miriam, but, in the meantime, you can't help but sing along.

Older graduates of teacher education programs vividly remember mandatory piano classes. For many, these are not fond memories, and are best left to cognitive decay lest they cause tremors and tingling sensations in the ears. The academic thought was that all teachers in Christian school classrooms needed piano skills to teach Jesus songs. Not a bad idea, but it totally ignored the reality that many teachers just didn't have a mote of Miriam in them.

With the departure of the piano phenomenon, the danger is that singing praise to God might disappear as well. We have plenty to sing and praise God about. Jesus came to save us. He defeated death for us. There's plenty for children to sing praises about. They just need someone to lead them. This is where you come in. Do you teach students to sing?

No fair pushing it off on music teachers. They have their own curricular agenda, but teaching music only during music class is like teaching religion only during religion class. What then about cross-curricular philosophy? You see, making the case for *you* to teach songs of praise is educationally sound.

If you haven't turned a tone-deaf ear toward this devotion yet, you still have hope.

As a means of encouragement and comfort, consider God's Word: "Let us come into His presence with thanksgiving; let us make a joyful noise to Him with songs of praise! For the Lord is a great God, and a great King above all gods" (Psalm 95:2–3).

No doubt, you are alert to the key phrase "joyful noise." Notice the absence of phrases like "Grammy winner" or "virtuoso performance." Not that those aren't welcome, but they are unnecessary. You can do it. If you can't find the official first note, most any will get you started. Or do what you do with technology challenges: Ask a student to start the song!

You'll need courage, but it probably isn't as essential for you as for the classroom across the hall. They should know your plans for making joyful noises. Of course, if you are shrewd (or seriously nervous), you'll buy a sound track accompaniment. Then sing. Or settle for making noise. Students should know old hymns and liturgical music. They should also learn contemporary songs that praise Jesus.

Okay, let's get going. When will you start? How will you start? How about a rousing hum of "Onward Christian Soldiers"? We can celebrate God's victories for His people just as Miriam did!

❖ **Background Reading:**
Exodus 15:1–21

13

Jabez

· · · · · · · · · · · · · · · ·

Jabez called upon the God of Israel, saying,
"Oh that You would bless me and enlarge my
border, and that Your hand might be with me."
(1 Chronicles 4:10a)

· · · · · · · · · · · · · · · ·

Imagine that Jabez is in your class. He is a collector. Jabez's accumulation of baseball cards, paper clips, and dead bugs clearly outclasses the collections of other boys. Jabez does not live for the moment; he sets his sights on better collections. He says, "When I grow up, I want to collect cash, stocks, and real estate." Jabez shuns many other things that preoccupy the thoughts of the other boys his age. He is the kind of budding entrepreneur that someone will write about centuries in the future.

Several years ago, *The Prayer of Jabez* was a popular book that suggested that praying the right prayer could result in wealth. God can do anything He wants, but not every prayer-to-riches-minded person will achieve his dream. Yet Jabez's brief story might do more than sell books. Does Jabez have anything to teach teachers?

(You're supposed to answer "yes.") Perhaps Jabez can help us think of collections aside from money. Ponder your collections.

You successfully collect sins, even without trying. You probably aren't proud of this collection, but it is the one possession of which you have excess. Unless, of course, you give it away. And that's precisely what you do. You give your sins to the only taker: Jesus Christ. His collection, compacted and compressed, would fill every tomb in the world. He earned none of them; He took all of them off sinners' hands.

That brings us to your second collection: forgiven sins. It's just as large as your first collection. It was a gift from your Brother, Jesus Christ. You would like to repay Him, but nobody could ever do that. Instead, you respond by dedicating your life in service to Him, and you follow His example.

Your students benefit from collections of their own. One is bestowed by you. Multiply the number of students in your room by, say, a conservatively estimated 150 sins per day, and you acquire a handsome collection of *forgiving* while they receive a complete collection of *forgiveness*. And that is what a Christian school is all about.

Jabez didn't make deals with God. He simply asked for wealth, and God gave it to him. The same is available to you and your students. It's all a matter of how you define *wealth*. Yours is a treasure chest filled with God's mercy and grace. It is priceless. Pray for more and more. And while you're at it, pray for those who are impoverished by a lack of faith or by a nomadic searching for better lives.

Feel free to give away your collection of mercy and grace. Unlike other riches, mercy and grace increase in your life the more you give them to others. You're probably a millionaire already!

❖ **Background Reading:**
1 Chronicles 4:9–10

14

Methuselah

. . . .

Methuselah lived after he fathered Lamech 782 years and had other sons and daughters. Thus all the days of Methuselah were 969 years, and he died. (Genesis 5:26–27)

. . . .

Imagine that Methuselah is in your class. He is in no hurry to move on. As he sees it, life is too long to hurry through anything. And if he must repeat a grade several times, he feels no pressure. After all, stress shortens life. Methuselah hopes to set a few records during his lifetime, but he doesn't feel compelled to expend any energy doing it.

Would you like to live as long as Methuselah? Once you passed 200 or 300, you might acclimate to the aches and pains. You might even see the Cubs win a World Series, if that is one of your goals. Your answer probably includes a condition, such as "If I had my health . . ." But of what importance was Methuselah that the Old Testament includes a few verses about him? Methuselah's importance is his place in the Savior's genealogy. He also fits the role of eye-popper when you tell students how long he lived!

What is Methuselah to you? Perhaps he provokes a few thoughts. Just what would you do if you lived 969 years? Here are some ideas:

- Tell stories about when gas was sold at filling stations.

- Show what a dollar looked like back when currency was used for trade.

- Revisit your old third-grade classroom to see if your favorite bulletin board is still hanging there.

Okay, so there are better things to do with life, and the longer your life, the more you can do. Think about all you have done just in the past year. How many ways have you served God through service to your students, their families, your congregation, and your friends and family? You probably can't count the ways. When service is part of your nature as a child of God, service experience isn't something you inventory. Service is a part of your life.

The trend in remaining on the job beyond 65 or 66 offers godly people additional opportunities to demonstrate and proclaim the Gospel. Whatever your age—and this is true for your students too—it's time that God provides for you to be a blessing to others.

Old age is more than a dream. You will have it. You'll have it longer than Methuselah had breath. You'll have it so long that time will become extinct. Jesus made that possible by forgiving your sins, having paid your penalty with His suffering and death and defeating death through His resurrection.

As you age, remember Methuselah. Enjoy God's ageless love. And don't worry if you have a few "Methuselah moments." It comes with age.

❖ **Background Reading:**
Genesis 5:21–27

15

Anna

. . . .

And coming up at that very hour she began to give thanks to God and to speak of Him to all who were waiting for the redemption of Jerusalem. (Luke 2:38)

. . . .

Imagine that Anna is in your class. She is the one—every school has one—who acts like the stereotypical little old grandma. She is comfortable waiting for a need to arise to which she can respond, shepherding distracted little boys and shy little girls, sharing her lunch with the hungry (or forgetful), and writing notes and prayers for classmates who are ill. Anna's patience and dedication to personal service make her popular among the other teachers and reliable help for students, who sometimes take advantage of her goodness.

The Bible calls the real Anna a *prophetess* who spent all her time in the temple. You may know the modern variety—the mom who stops by every day to see if the office needs some help. She is the one who signs up to chaperone field trips and volunteers for the most "difficult" group. She is in Bible class, serves on the altar guild, and cooks for youth fund-raisers. And she is the one who greets families after the Baptism of their children. (Then she writes down the family's name in a small journal so she will remember to pray for them.) She might be a *he*, and it might even be you.

A ministry of patient presence normally attracts no salary and needs little training; but it does require lots of thoughtfulness. Teachers often believe that the tasks for which they are trained fall in the realm of professional service, intentionally performed with strongly relational practices. But the best teachers are a little like Anna—though they shouldn't be in the "temple" all the time! To be the best you can be, consider the following.

First, focus on the Savior. All your classroom goodness and professionalism flow from the cross where Jesus died for your sins. They are gifts of the Holy Spirit that you generously use as you await the coming of Jesus.

Second, focus on the Savior. Were you to stop teaching tomorrow, you would retain all the characteristics of a teacher, and although you could refocus your activities, you would not ever want to change the object of your affection—Jesus Christ.

Third, focus on the Savior. Consider all that you do a fleeting pastime, a minute hash mark on the eternal timeline. Serving the Savior at your school, for example, should not keep you from family and friends in ways that destroy or diminish God-given earthly relationships. Your focus on the Savior also involves godly relationships at home, as you relate and interact in the name of and under the influence of the Savior.

Anna lived with the promise of a Savior; she saw that promise fulfilled that day when Mary and Joseph entered the temple. You live with a promise too. You already know that the Savior has come. (If you've ever been to even one school Christmas program, you've heard this promise!) Now you live with the promise of His second coming. Maybe it will be tomorrow, or maybe it will be when you are very much older. Perhaps you'll be resting in the grave when He comes again. But one thing is sure—or make that two: Jesus will return. And you'll be as happy as Anna when you see Him for the first time.

❖ **Background Reading:**
Luke 2:36–38

16

Nehemiah

· · · · · · · · · · · · · · · ·

*"But if you return to Me and keep My command-
ments and do them, though your outcasts are
in the uttermost parts of heaven, from there I
will gather them and bring them to the place that
I have chosen, to make My name dwell there."
They are Your servants and Your people, whom
You have redeemed by Your great power and by
Your strong hand. (Nehemiah 1:9–10)*

· · · · · · · · · · · · · · · ·

Imagine that Nehemiah is in your class. He
quietly goes about his studies and socializing.
Underlying his daily work and play is a deep passion for classmates. If, on a rare occasion, you
mistakenly reprimand an innocent student—or
even one whose behavior and discipline must be
understood as circumstances beyond his control,
Nehemiah, without appearing rebellious, will see
you privately to provide insight and seek your
blessing for him to show compassion.

Too bad a reading of the Book of Nehemiah doesn't provide Continuing Education Credits. Teachers, open to a little creative thinking, could walk away as improved professionals.

As Nehemiah's Book opens, he is absorbed by an activity that is essential to imitate: repentance. It's really not natural. In perspective of your school, how often do complaints spin out of control? For example, the heat is too hot or the air conditioning is too cold, the chalkboards are wearing thin or the interactive whiteboards have a stupid day, or the clock in your room is thirteen seconds off. The principal is probably to blame, or let's pin the tail of blame on the janitor. Or somebody else.

Then there are other problems: sinful students, families, staff, boards, *et al.* They can be as broken as Jerusalem's walls back in Nehemiah's era. Whose fault is it when students don't understand an assignment or fail to turn in their work? Who is to blame when the apple that doesn't fall far from the tree is wormy and bruised? Whose fault is it when . . . well, the list is too long to write.

Some solutions may be within your grasp, so if you are not part of the solution, then you are part of the problem. (Sin works very well that way.) And that brings you to repentance, Nehemiah style.

Nehemiah was concerned about the spiritual condition of people, namely the people who pretty much brought the problems on themselves through failure to fear, love, and trust God. Nehemiah included his own family in the culpability. So where do you fit in this?

You may or may not have direct responsibility for the ills of your school or congregation or those you serve. But you are numbered in the throng of God's people—true believers, mind you—who sin regularly. Therefore, repentance is appropriate even if you—you've heard this one before—don't know what you did. Fortunately, God remains in the business of forgiving. Jesus paid the price to make forgiveness possible and to lead us to repent so that we might receive it.

Repentance leads to restoration. Confessed sin leads to absolution. Absolution leads to new zeal for repairing lives, if not HVAC systems. You are your students' and your schools' daily Nehemiah. God is with you, and you have a lifetime of needs to meet. God bless your work. Now get busy!

❖ **Background Reading:**
   Nehemiah 1:11b–2:8

17

Noah

. . . .

God blessed Noah and his sons and said to them, "Be fruitful and multiply and fill the earth." (Genesis 9:1)

. . . .

Imagine that Noah is in your class. Noah's classmates consider him "a little strange." His out-of-the-box thinking has led him to a hobby of fishing, though the nearest place to fish and actually catch something is 300 miles away. You see him at recess, armed with a fly rod. He practices roll casts until he can snag a kindergartner's snack at 30 yards! Upon questioning, you find that Noah has little interest in actually catching fish. He loves animals and expresses interest in becoming a pet shop proprietor. Obedience is another of Noah's fortes.

Thinking about a Noahlike student invites uncomplimentary comparisons of classrooms to the ark and students to various animals with whom they share some . . . er . . . characteristics. But that is not the goal, even though you could make a case for such comparisons. Your school is filled with children saved by Jesus! Instead, consider the real Noah's relationship with God.

God's anger at the people whom He loved but who didn't return the love—or even loyalty—was storming toward disastrous consequences. Noah and his family emerged as the only righteous people on Earth! This was not due to Noah's behavior; it was the result of God's work with Noah. And that's the first lesson.

If Jesus returned today, would He find you and your students righteous? Even out of sight of the teacher at recess? Even in the faculty lounge? Even . . . well, you get the idea.

You are righteous. So are all the young believers in your classroom. As with Noah, you didn't get that way through your own merit. Jesus made you righteous through His life, death, and resurrection. Were Jesus to return today, have no doubt that God would find you righteous and welcome in heaven.

Please be sure that your students know they are righteous independent of themselves. One student remembers a misguided (though sincere) Christian teacher who suggested that if you went horseback riding on Sunday morning instead of going to church, and the horse threw and trampled you to death, you would go to hell—and it wouldn't be on horseback! While such stories attempt to emphasize the importance of worship, they also lead those who attend church to think that such activity makes them righteous. We owe our righteousness to Jesus, who died to save us from our sins once and for all times.

Back to another lesson from Noah: obedience. How silly it seemed to build a boat where there were no observable resources in which to launch it. Imagine the derision and irritation of his neighbors over this lengthy project! But nothing could deter Noah. He followed God's command, even though it seemed to make no sense.

You do the same thing. You teach about Jesus. How silly it must seem to outsiders, especially highly educated outsiders, when you talk about true God and true man, about perfect life, about sacrificing life for friends and enemies alike, and then—topping the incredibility charts—coming back to life again.

Skeptics and scoffers can stop you no more than they stopped Noah. You sail under the same power that he did.

❖ **Background Reading:**
Genesis 6:5–22

18

Philip

. . . .

And the Spirit said to Philip, "Go over and join this chariot." So Philip ran to him and heard him reading Isaiah the prophet and asked, "Do you understand what you are reading?" And he said, "How can I, unless someone guides me?" And he invited Philip to come up and sit with him. (Acts 8:29–31)

. . . .

Imagine that Philip is in your class. You never know where you'll find him. He is your track star, never walking, always running from place to place. Teachers know him for his willingness to tutor classmates. He may also be inclined to chase cars, seeing if he can keep up with them—and often startling drivers as he comes close.

The apostle Philip wasted no time in telling others about Jesus. In the Bible's most famous account of him, the Holy Spirit sends him chariot chasing, pursuing a government official who was reading God's Word but having no clear understanding of the subject. Anyone can read the words of the Bible; it takes faith to accept and understand them.

For whom is there such urgency in your classroom? You can't tell for sure, and the Holy Spirit isn't going to whisk you over to that desk. You know which students have a church home and how often they use it. Yet that knowledge is no guarantee of who needs your Christian instruction and testimony most. You simply cannot accurately judge such things.

A sense of urgency surrounds all your students. You don't know who will be back in class tomorrow or next year. Since you have experienced God's love through Jesus Christ, you don't need much time to prepare your message. Show and tell students each day what it means to have faith in the Savior who moved out of heaven so He could suffer on earth, pay for the sins of the world with His life, and then rise from the dead in victory over the death and the devil.

You have much the same role with your students as Philip did with the Ethiopian. Due to unbelief or age, they will find the Bible difficult reading. (Due to lack of experience or study, you may share that experience!) You will need to explain what they read through faith-based study and scholarship. What baffles you upon reading a selection from Scripture? The answer to that question will lead you to research—and the joy of learning something new about the God who loves you. (As if there were any other!)

As you explain and clarify God's Word, be sure to look for Jesus. It is easy to miss Him—even in the book that is about Him! Bible stories, for example, often do not mention the Savior's name or the story's niche in the history of salvation. The story of David and Goliath is a childhood favorite, but it is often told as little more than a story of good triumphing over evil at great risk and odds. The villain is Goliath. The hero is David. But that's not the whole story. Students need to understand that God was behind the incident. Not only was David killing God's enemy but he was also keeping alive the family into which Jesus would be born.

Baptism provides another example. Philip's story reports how he baptized the Ethiopian—and the reason for it. Students, both baptized and not (yet), need to know that God's victory in winning them is as dramatic as the fatal knockout blow to Goliath. God has defeated the devil's attempt to kill them. They are part of God's family.

❖ **Background Reading:**
Acts 8:26–39

60

19

Isaiah

· · · · · · · · · · · · · · · ·

*Who has measured the waters in the hollow
of His hand and marked off the heavens with
a span, enclosed the dust of the earth in a
measure and weighed the mountains in scales
and the hills in a balance? (Isaiah 40:12)*

· · · · · · · · · · · · · · · ·

Imagine that Isaiah is in your class. He keeps
everything in perspective. Worldly facts and data
do not impress him. High mountains, vast oceans,
and great works of literature and music are an
emphatic ho-hum with Isaiah, but he possesses a
forthright conviction that the Creator is magnifi-
cently higher, wider, and deeper than His creation.
Some classmates think that Isaiah has an overac-
tive imagination; he argues that nothing imagined
can come close to God in all His glory!

Education sometimes gets too full of itself.
Knowledge increases every day. Research, en-
hanced by technology, enables discoveries and
developments never before imagined. Thinkers,

tinkerers, and theorists become more confident in their abilities, moving forward from an ever-increasing base of background knowledge.

You are a teacher. It's likely that you love learning, that you always want to know more and teach more. And, as a Bible-believing teacher, you learn about God from Isaiah to keep knowledge in perspective. Let's review a few features of this godly perspective from Isaiah 40.

- Verse 12a: "Who has measured the waters in the hollow of His hand." That is one humongous hand! Millions of words have contributed explanations and hypotheses about the oceans, lakes, and rivers of the world. Should your students know what Isaiah wrote? You might need to add that to the state standards!

- Verse 12b: "Marked off the heavens with a span." God's hand remains the subject here, but now the focus is on its width. The United States has spent billions of dollars on the Hubble space telescope to discover our origins and more. Remind students that a cheap Bible provides that information in the very first chapter. And then thank God for the Hubble. It continues to generate reasons to praise God for His power and glory.

- Verse 15: "Behold, the nations are like a drop from a bucket." The weight of most social studies textbooks and the length of social commentaries seem like a whole lot more than a drop from a bucket! History's record of power struggles and empires evokes both awe and fear in our hearts. Mockeries of justice are commonplace, and enormous effort works to maintain separation of God from people. Social injustice may anger students, but remind them that what the people of our world do has no effect on the realities of God. He will continue to be faithful to His people.

One reason to teach Scripture and faith across the curriculum is to keep us—all we know and all we will know—in perspective. As old sets of *Encyclopedia Britannica* hold only a fraction of today's knowledge, what we know today is only a fraction of what we don't know—what God hasn't yet uncovered for us. But of all the things we know and will discover, the most important thing is this: Jesus is our Savior. That puts everything in happy perspective.

❖ **Background Reading:**
Isaiah 40

20

Leah

· · · · · · · · · · · · · · · ·

Leah's eyes were weak. (Genesis 29:17)

· · · · · · · · · · · · · · · ·

Imagine that Leah is in your class. She sits in the front row. (Leah has a sister, Rachel, in a younger class; the sisters are quite different.) You wonder what Leah's parents were thinking when they named her. Had they checked a name-the-baby book, they would have learned that *Leah* means "weary." And her name aptly describes her physical appearance, especially her eyes, which look perpetually tired. But appearance isn't every-thing (except to those who lack grace and beauty). Good work habits and ambition are important for success. Leah strikes you as headed for a success-ful life—shrouded by brooding unhappiness. Dear teacher, watch for the Leahs in your class. You don't need much more description than that which appears in this first paragraph. Name your Leah or Leahs in your mind right now.

What can Leah teach you? Were you—are you ever—like her? Does *weary* describe you? Sin is a major cause of weariness. Sin would have driven a wedge between you and Jesus, had He not sacrificed His life to make you His figurative Bride.

Consider your life with the divine Bridegroom, Jesus Christ. Yes, consider this even if you are male; *Bridegroom* and *Bride* talk are metaphors for Jesus and believers. The Bridegroom requires a perfect Bride. In that respect, every sinner is a lot like Leah. But, unlike Leah's husband, Jacob, Jesus is the perfect Bridegroom. Praise God! Jesus loves all people. He loves you with a passion more intense than Jacob's passion for Leah's beautiful sister, Rachel. Jesus doesn't love you because you have bright eyes; He loves you because He *is* love.

God blessed the biblical Leah. She and Jacob had many children. Now that's another thing to make you weary! And it offers another parallel for you and Leah.

How many children has God given you to serve? How far does your responsibility extend? State standards, important as they are, don't embrace all your responsibilities. You must teach faith, and teaching faith requires knowledge and application of Scripture. Faith must permeate your classroom not only during religion class but also throughout the day. Teaching and practicing the faith never end. More to make you weary!

Good thing God strengthens you. He sends the Holy Spirit to aid you in your important mission. You say you haven't noticed? Sometimes the Spirit's work may be obvious, but often it is seamless. The Spirit works within you to help you serve your students. Whenever you tell students that Jesus loves them, that's evidence of your faith, uttered by the power of the Spirit, and working through Word and Sacrament.

Whatever your weaknesses, whatever makes you weary, doesn't matter to Jesus. He took your burdens upon Himself, carried them to the cross, and dumped them there to rot with all the other sins of the world. You need not carry that which makes you weary. Turn it over to Jesus. He is your Friend.

Say . . . do the words *Jesus* and *Friend* in the same sentence remind you of any hymns? Too bad Leah couldn't sing that one on her weary days. But you don't share Leah's lack of hymnody. Why not take a few moments to sing it now? (You can find it in CPH's *Lutheran Service Book* as hymn 770.)

❖ **Background Reading:**
Genesis 29:1–30

21

David

. . . .

For I know my transgressions, and my sin is ever before me. (Psalm 51:3)

. . . .

Imagine that David is in your class. He is an athlete, poet, and musician. His magnetic personality makes him popular with girls and boys alike. He is protective and loyal, though he suffers bouts of bad judgment. He is the one most likely to be named Class Hero.

If you teach younger children, or if you have earned popularity with older ones, you are their hero. Of course, you are their hero even if they don't think that way. Teachers of all varieties— early childhood, elementary, secondary, youth group, Sunday School, VBS, volunteer or paid— are heroes. You don't slay lions or slaughter Philistines. You fight the forces of ignorance and beat back the enemies of faith. You sacrifice your own comfort and make hundreds of critical judgments every day. Yes, that's the stuff of heroism.

David demonstrated the characteristics of a hero. Better yet, he demonstrated the nature of a godly hero. Students learn of his deeds, both tragic and victorious. You teach the stories of how his music soothed the violent fits of a king and how his respect for God prevented him from killing the king who wanted to kill him. Sounds like the good-guy-in-the-white-hat sort of hero, right?

David teaches us that all heroes are also fallen heroes. The Bible graphically exposes the hero's sins to the extent that his hero status is not only tarnished but also deserves to be stripped from him. Does your hero status tip and teeter? Does your heart well up with a sense of relief that the Bible doesn't mention your name?

You share the hero characteristics of David. You know your sins—things you would never confess to your students or share with parents or include in your bio. You also know the futility of trying to hide those flaws from God. He knows. He knows exactly what kind of hero you are. But then there is this, courtesy of a Spirit-inspired David:

"Create in me a clean heart, O God, and renew a right spirit within me. . . . The sacrifices of God are a broken spirit; a broken and contrite heart, O God, You will not despise" (Psalm 51:10, 17).

Real heroes repent. Aware of their sinfulness, they take their condition to God, ask His forgiveness, and seek His strength to avoid sin. God listens, not because the heroes have earned status, but because He sent His Son to pay for the sins of heroes. Cowards too. And all in between. God sends His Spirit to equip heroes not with swords and slingshots but with faith.

You probably don't think of yourself as a hero in the image of David. You probably don't think of yourself as a hero in any image at all. And that's exactly what makes you a hero, because behind you stands the only perfect Hero—the one who died. The one who rose. The one who is with you every day.

❖ **Background Reading:**
Psalm 119

22

Zacchaeus

• • • • • • • • • • • • • • • •

And he [Zacchaeus] was seeking to see who Jesus was, but on account of the crowd he could not, because he was small of stature. (Luke 19:3)

• • • • • • • • • • • • • • • •

Imagine that Zacchaeus is in your class. You must watch him closely. Zacchaeus is sneaky and a top suspect in most classroom infractions, but there is rarely sufficient evidence to pin the trouble on him. He likes to cheat too. Most of his academic recognitions are not supported by rigorous study. Mothers order their children to stay away from Zacchaeus, for nobody trusts him. Some parents (and even a teacher) have suggested that Zacchaeus doesn't belong in a Christian school classroom. He certainly doesn't act as Christians do! Teachers pick up "street smarts" by way of Zacchaeus.

Luke puts Zacchaeus at center stage for a good view of the Savior. Perhaps due to his height, students relate to Zacchaeus. Though short, he wanted to see Jesus, who was gaining prominence.

Zacchaeus teaches you not to give up before you start. It's a valuable lesson to help you reach kids in your class who take unfair advantage of you and their classmates. But their mischief is more a decoy than the real thing. They listen, and therein exists your opportunity. They hear every word you say about Jesus, and the Spirit works curiosity in their conniving little hearts. Given the opportunity, they seek to see Jesus.

You are the next best thing.

You minister to your class in the name of Jesus. The Spirit equips you to model Jesus' behavior, but sometimes Satan distracts you. Satan sees Jesus as a demanding Lawgiver. This is a natural hazard for teachers too. You live and teach moral manners, perhaps implying—unintentionally—that Christlike behavior is the ultimate human expression of devout Christianity.

The New Testament Gospels, taken out of context, support Satan's charade. They contain lots of Law, as Jesus repeatedly reveals the kind of behavior God expects. Attempted obedience results in either smug self-righteousness or doleful despair. And there is middle ground too. Some "law-abiding" individuals make an outward show of obeying God while hiding—in vain, mind you—their guilt. They labor under the delusion that hiding their sin is as good as obeying the rules.

Modeling Jesus to students involves more than living by high moral standards.

Modeling Jesus involves compassion, mercy, grace, forgiveness, and even risk. As Jesus risked His reputation by dining with corrupt (but repentant!) Zacchaeus, you can seek opportunities to build a relationship with kids who aren't openly interested in learning of Jesus' love. Have lunch with the "outcasts" too. Your unconditional love can chip away hardness and disperse apathy. Jesus' love changes lives as it saves them.

It would be gratifying to see a change in your students as Jesus saw in the demonstrably repentant Zacchaeus. You may or may not have that privilege. Or it might surface in trivial ways—acts of kindness or helpfulness toward you that are insignificant but not insincere.

Now as you march into your classroom, thank God for the students who are already in their expected places. But look for the kid who is out on a limb; see if he will share his snack with you.

❖ **Background Reading:**
Luke 19:2–10

23

Ethel

· · · · · · · · · · · · · · · ·

Now there are also many other things that Jesus did. Were every one of them to be written, I suppose that the world itself could not contain the books that would be written. (John 21:25)

· · · · · · · · · · · · · · · ·

Imagine that Ethel is in your class. She is difficult to imagine because you rarely notice her. She is nondescript and transparent, blending in to most situations so well that she becomes easy to ignore. She does not participate in class discussions, giggle at your silly jokes, defy the dress code, or complain when bad weather dampens recess plans.

Okay, so Ethel isn't any more noticeable in the Bible than she is in your classroom. She is too ordinary to make the book. While you will not find her name in Scripture, Ethel-types certainly were among Jesus' followers. He noticed them even when others did not.

Since you teach in a Christian classroom, you seek and find your own anonymous Ethels. Proceed with caution; urging them away from their comfort zone may not be what they want. They want you to care for and notice them and to show the love Jesus has for the shy and those who prefer the Ethel life. They want to hear how Jesus lived, died, and rose to take away their sins. They may be pleased with an invitation to become more noticeable without actually having to do so.

Sadly, the devil hates the Ethels as much as Jesus loves them. The stronger his hate, the more attractive the intended victim. So the battles for Ethel's soul rage as intensely as they do for any child. You can't be a disinterested bystander, for that makes you an accomplice of the devil. You need to pray, teach, and witness. Ethel needs you. Or maybe you need Ethel.

Do you enjoy teaching? Why? (This paragraph is short, so you have time to answer.)

You enjoy helping students discover new facts, ideas, and dreams. You find serving students congruent with how you perceive your Christian vocational role. You can even see yourself proclaiming the Gospel in a mission field close to home. You consider yourself blessed.

Your joy focuses on the triumphs you can observe—the students whose enthusiasm you've awakened or those "beasts" whom you have civilized. Then there is Ethel, who leaves the same way she came. Perhaps you've coaxed a smile from her or spied a glimmer in her eyes or watched a little bounce in her step. However, it is what happened within her soul that matters. She has grown in Christ because she was with you. How can you know? Here is what you will see (God says so):

"For as the rain and the snow come down from heaven and do not return there but water the earth, making it bring forth and sprout, giving seed to the sower and bread to the eater, so shall My word be that goes out from My mouth; it shall not return to Me empty, but it shall accomplish that which I purpose, and shall succeed in the thing for which I sent it. For you shall go out in joy and be led forth in peace; the mountains and the hills before you shall break forth into singing, and all the trees of the field shall clap their hands" (Isaiah 55:10–12).

Say, isn't that Ethel over there, clapping with the mountains?

24

Deborah

. . . .

*And she said, "I will surely go with you. Never-theless, the road on which you are going will not lead to your glory, for the L*ORD *will sell Sisera into the hand of a woman." Then Deborah arose and went with Barak to Kedesh. (Judges 4:9)*

. . . .

Imagine that Deborah is in your class. Even the tougher boys look up to her. (Of course, *tougher* often translates to *insecure*.) She is the one who hides around the corner to scare the boys as they come by. Deborah has a flair for rallying to the aid of classmates, usually with her fists clenched and her body poised for conflict. In pre-political-correctness days, she might have been called a tomboy, which probably wouldn't have mattered to her—and if it did, you would know about it. Quickly. Maybe painfully. Deborah's confidence is rooted in knowing how God has gifted her. Her brutal honesty can be offensive, but it is indeed honesty. The class prophecy predicts a career in the justice system.

Female teachers reading this might not realize that many years ago they would not be reading this. Women were not found teaching in early Christian school classrooms. In a sense, then, they share a little history with Deborah, who was commissioned to be a judge at a time when she was not of the gender selected for titled leadership. Deborah's story offers something to think about.

Deborah was among a minority of religious leadership. The leadership of women is vital to the future of the Christian Church. Do not fool yourself or allow yourself to be fooled. You are a vital dynamic in Christian education, and the Holy Spirit works through you as you proclaim the Word and integrate faith into everything you teach.

You also are instrumental in the war against evil, as was Deborah. She didn't stand on the sidelines and watch. She took charge and issued orders in the name of God. You do that too, right?

Your orders take on language that differs from Deborah's, but its effects are just as just! What orders do you issue?

- Behave yourself! This may be the most common order uttered in any school day. Well-managed classrooms contribute to learning and discipline that align with God's will.

- Practice mercy! This is far more difficult than demanding moral behavior, for mercy is the requisite reaction to those who struggle with behavior. Patience accompanies mercy and releases opportunities for transformative behavior in response to Jesus' love.

- Start fresh. Armed with God's response to daily repentance, you and your students are forgiven by Jesus and free to serve as God's children.

Biblical Deborah was famous as a wise judge and a remarkably bold military advisor. You probably don't think of how people will remember you—and even if you do, it is okay!

Your legacy will be that of a judge, because that is the nature of teachers. Pray that your legacy also is one of fairness, wisdom, and courage. Most of all, pray that you'll be remembered for what happened to you and what you did so freely for those whom you serve: forgiven to forgive.

❖ **Background Reading:**
   Judges 4:4–24

25

Judas

．．．．．．．．．．．．．．．．

Now the betrayer had given them a sign, saying,
"The one I will kiss is the man; seize Him."
(Matthew 26:48)

．．．．．．．．．．．．．．．．

Imagine that Judas is in your class. It's not your fault; every teacher has one. Judas looks to turn situations to his advantage. On rainy days, he rents his umbrella to hapless classmates. If you need a class treasurer for the fund-raiser, Judas is your eager volunteer. You can count on him to undertake many projects, and you count on him to benefit from his beneficence. Judas does seem to have a conscience, though. Mostly a guilty one. Not that he doesn't contend with it. He seems prone to punishing himself.

Biblical Judas makes you want to cry. His betrayal of Jesus produces anger. His suicide produces tears. You may have someone like him in your classroom. You may share some Judas genes yourself. What can you do?

Do you have a deeply private sin, one of which you frequently repent but can never forget? Perhaps you don't name the sin because of the shame it incites. Perhaps you even suspect that none of your students harbors guilt feelings like yours. You don't want to talk about it. Not even with God. Jesus has forgiven you, as you have asked. You just can't forgive yourself.

You have students that feel that way, especially if they are older. Their sinfulness has clamped bear-trap jaws on their souls. Though you have told them about their Savior, they just can't break loose from sin's guilt trap.

You are a teacher for times like these—your own and your students. You know what Jesus did for you, and you must teach separation of knowledge and feelings. You must learn and teach the objective fact of forgiveness earned by Jesus. You must talk about how Jesus took away your sins regardless of guilt's remnant, which usually occupies a disconsolate edge of your soul.

Words aren't enough to accomplish acceptance of complete forgiveness. Your behavior substantiates what you teach. The forgiveness you share and proclaim with students must also infiltrate your smile, your casual conversations, your eyes, and your tone of voice. In the end, students will decide for themselves if they will accept forgiveness—or even think they need it. At some point, you realize that you don't have control over how students react. What can you do?

If you've ever had a student or a friend who committed suicide or who exhibits spiritual despair or stubborn unbelief, you likely have mourned. Maybe you've felt guilty, as if somehow you didn't do enough—or maybe did too much. You forget that God allows free will, even to the point of self-destruction. And you wonder why.

Wondering may instigate philosophical musings without producing concrete answers. We just don't understand spiritual mysteries, especially those that leave scars. In the end, you must simply live with the pain. Oh, it dulls, but it never goes away. But that's only a feeling, however strong. You live with facts. And the fact is that God doesn't hold you responsible for the sins of others, and He has already taken away all of yours.

That's enough to make Satan leap into the chasm between heaven and hell.

> ❖ **Background Reading:**
> Matthew 26:14–27:10

26

Thomas

. . . .

Unless I see in His hands the mark of the nails,
and place my finger into the mark of the nails,
and place my hand into His side, I will never
believe. (John 20:25)

. . . .

Imagine that Thomas is in your class. During his preschool years, Thomas nagged his teacher by asking "Why?" about everything. He is now the one who demands proof for everything you teach, which probably is a scholarly asset but sometimes is offensive, because it sounds like a rude challenge rather than legitimate curiosity. Other students tire of it too. Thomas will discover a vocation in which his questions will help him succeed.

How sad that Christians remember Thomas more for his doubt than his faith. You, however, being a compassionate teacher, can probably relate, both with sympathy and empathy—tinged with a little disappointment.

Teachers want students to believe them. Jesus, the Master Teacher, expected trust from His disciples but was often disappointed by their failure to grasp His nature. You know the feeling.

Did your teachers know the feeling too? Some of you are hanging your heads right now, while others think they have a righteous answer. Both reactions are valid. Both can help you be even better teachers than you are right now.

Sin plays a significant role in your ability to teach. You are a sinner. Your students are sinners. Therefore, you share a natural connection. What does that do for you?

Perhaps your own sinfulness helps you understand the conflict sin causes in kids. Maybe you understand their temptations more because you've faced—and fallen—to similar enticements. That doesn't place your students in good company, but it does open the door to forgiveness. It also opens the door to godly counsel, teacher-to-student (and student-to-teacher?), on fighting temptation when it arises again.

The unnatural consequence of sin is forgiveness. The Bible made clear the relationship between God and sinners: It was broken and hostile. The natural consequence was abandonment by God and eternal punishment in hell. Ah, but you know forgiveness. Sweet, sweet forgiveness. You share it with your students too. Sounds like your classroom is a *bona fide* Saint and Sinner City.

Mutually beneficial relationships may be the norm, but forgiveness is hard. You can't always determine why you can't penetrate hard hearts or sluggish minds. Sometimes you care so much for your students that the relationship breeds anger or bitterness. Your greatest worry may relate to faith: Do your students believe in Jesus? Yes, they say they do, but judging by their behavior, well, you may doubt it. (Whoops! Did I really say "judging" by their behavior?)

Be comforted. Jesus did not treat weak or even missing faith with a zero-tolerance attitude. For Thomas, the Holy Spirit provided opportunity to prove Jesus' case. Thomas did not have blind faith. He needed help. He got it. And for you and your students, faith sometimes wavers, but that isn't fatal. The smallest particle of faith results in salvation. That small seed of faith can grow sturdy and strong as you study and share God's Word.

Will you ever tire of hearing what Jesus did for you? I doubt it.

❖ **Background Reading:**
    John 20:24–29

27

Naboth

· · · · · · · · · · · · · · ·

And the two worthless men came in and sat opposite him. And the worthless men brought a charge against Naboth in the presence of the people, saying, "Naboth cursed God and the king." So they took him outside the city and stoned him to death with stones. Then they sent to Jezebel, saying, "Naboth has been stoned; he is dead." As soon as Jezebel heard that Naboth had been stoned and was dead, Jezebel said to Ahab, "Arise, take possession of the vineyard of Naboth the Jezreelite, which he refused to give you for money, for Naboth is not alive, but dead." (1 Kings 21:13–15)

· · · · · · · · · · · · · · ·

Imagine that Naboth is in your class. It's almost as if he wears a big target on the back of his shirt. He is the one who would be unanimously voted and loudly proclaimed winner of the most vulnerable student in the room. The only students to really love him are the bullies. Naboth tolerates relentless emotional and physical torment. His solace is in the little school garden where the science class grows beans and zucchini. Out of your earshot, kids call Naboth names. You wonder how long he can take the abuse. (Jezebel is his most heartless adversary.)

Maybe you don't want to read this devotion. If you know Naboth's story, you know the tragic ending, so willingly and wickedly orchestrated by Jezebel. This is not an uplifting devotion, but you know the potential havoc that bullies inflict on others. You never want that to happen in your class.

Bullies are an old phenomenon. They assimilate their era's resources. Today, technology facilitates high-speed and broad-range access for shredding the vulnerable. And yes, it even happens in Christian schools and congregations. The devil takes more pleasure than normal when it happens among Christians and within their organizations.

As with all sin, you are powerless to prevent it. Don't feel bad. Sin cannot be drowned, burned, starved, legislated, or sacrificed out of existence. Its practice cannot be eradicated until Jesus comes again to take us to heaven. None of this is to advocate a nonchalant attitude toward sin. You have two weapons against sin in this present life.

The first is *forgiveness*. Forgiveness can be nearly impossible when it involves bullies. They often think they don't need it and will laugh in the face of confrontation. They will not repent. They delight in their relational perversity. Often, they intend to maim psyches, without calculating their potential to destroy physical life. Yes, they are hard to forgive. In all of history, Jesus seems the only one who could do that, asking God the Father's mercy on His killers even as He was dying.

The second weapon is *prayer*. Pray for the bullied; pray for the bullies. Then get busy. Get busy being the answer to your own prayers. You cannot tolerate bullying. You need to intervene. You need to confront the bullies and comfort the bullied. You need to work with other professionals who specialize in therapy. You need to speak with parents, who may fail to recognize the potential of their own children's brutality. Perhaps you will face some bullies yourself.

❖ **Background Reading:**
1 Kings 21:1–27

28

Timothy

· · · · · · · · · · · · · · · ·

I am reminded of your sincere faith, a faith that dwelt first in your grandmother Lois and your mother Eunice and now, I am sure, dwells in you as well. (2 Timothy 1:5)

· · · · · · · · · · · · · · · ·

Imagine that Timothy is in your class. He has a "good family" who supports him through encouragement, discipline, and, most of all, teaching the faith. They support you too, as you teach God's word—both Law and Gospel! Timothy benefits from family/teacher collaboration, an asset that seems more rare each year. You enjoy Timothy's presence.

Your work would be much easier if you didn't need to undo all the hooey that impedes educational progress. Research suggests that education's effectiveness increases when parents are active in their children's education and when they perceive a partnership with the school in raising their children.

Leave it to sin to corrupt that excellent concept! Parental involvement mutates into pressure from parents to make their children happy, even if it means sacrificing standards or behavioral expectations. Or maybe the mess comes from colleagues who insist that all children must learn the same way, regardless of developmental levels or learning styles. Oh, where are Eunice and Lois when you need them?

While many of the families you deal with are helpful and perceptive, others are apathetic—or worse. The apathetic don't bother you much, but they don't interact beneficially with their children either. Their sinfulness is silent and easily ignored. Results of apathy may not show up for years, but, as a children's advocate, you need to encourage and instruct these parents. You need to lavish them with the same gift God gave you: patient grace!

Gulp! Now consider those, even if few, who occupy the largest amount of consciousness, time, and eardrum vibrations:

You know they dislike you, and you could live with that if only they recognized all that you do for their children. You agonize over their accusations, which often have a single, miniscule molecule of truth—enough to make you feel partially responsible for whatever the current dilemma is.

And they seem to have a new dilemma for most days of the month, including weekends and holidays. Yes, you need to work hard with them too. After all, God sent their children to you too.

Whenever you find yourself shaking your head in disgust—or some other emotion—remember your relationship with the Master Teacher. The unmerciful truth is that you share several characteristic of poor parents and churlish children.

You have not been cooperative with God the Father, God the Son, or God the Holy Spirit! The all-powerful God—don't get upset now—does not need you. But He does want you. God loved you so much that He became true man to pay for your sins—without your asking. Having sacrificed His life for you, He sent His Holy Spirit to give you faith and to sanctify your life and service to Him. He did all this without collaboration, policies, or any glimmer of skill or talent on your part. God is the only true manifestation of an extraordinary parent. Praise God for being the Father of all fathers.

By the way, He will work with you and His other children. He already did the most important thing. He will help with the "little" stuff too.

❖ **Background Reading:**
2 Timothy 1:1–11

29

Solomon

. . . .

*In that night God appeared to Solomon, and
said to him, "Ask what I shall give you."*
(2 Chronicles 1:7)

. . . .

Imagine that Solomon is in your class. (If you
need more uplifting, imagine seven more like him!)
Solomon is the one for whom you have the high-
est standards, and he meets them all—adding a
healthy dose of wisdom along the way. His humility parallels his leadership, and every teacher after
you dreamily anticipates his presence. As for you,
finding a way to retain him would be top priority,
were it not totally selfish. Yet, something about
Solomon bothers you. You can't put your finger
on the source of your glum misgiving, but you fear
that the young man's wisdom will someday lead to
skepticism and maybe even depression.

What would you do if God offered you anything for the asking?

Such a consideration may appear, at first thought, tantamount to asking what you would buy if you won the lottery. But winning a lottery is a case for pure probability; God's offers are sure. So . . . for what would you ask?

You might realize that you already have everything you need. And you didn't even ask for it! God chose you, before you were born, to receive the gift of faith in Jesus, your Savior. You have the promise of eternal life as you live with God Himself. You can't figure out why God did this, and that makes you even more grateful. The righteousness Jesus purchased on the cross enables His invitation, "Ask what I shall give you."

If you read the background verses, you know that Solomon asked to lead God's people with skill and wisdom. God liked Solomon's request. It "took the cake"—so much so that God put lots of frosting on it! Solomon's wealth and wisdom were without parallel.

Let's make this devotion interactive. What three things would you request if God offered you anything for the asking?

1.

2.

3.

How certain are you that God will grant your petitions or intercessions? Oh, you know that God is no genie in a lamp who grants whims and wishes. God wants us to ask for spiritual blessings, and He promises to grant them—in ways that are best for you and those for whom you pray. Sometimes those spiritual blessings are accompanied by physical blessings too. And sometimes not. But spiritual blessings always lead to contentment and trust that God always provides what you need.

Your students have many needs. Are some not baptized? Are some floundering in their faith? Do some reject Jesus? Are others obviously filled with faith? They all need to be on your prayer list.

Let's go interactive again. Take time now to name each student in a prayer. And may God give you the wisdom of Solomon.

> ❖ **Background Reading:**
> **2 Chronicles 1:1–12**

30

Ruth

. . . .

But Ruth said, "Do not urge me to leave you or to return from following you. For where you go I will go, and where you lodge I will lodge. Your people shall be my people, and your God my God." (Ruth 1:16)

. . . .

Imagine that Ruth is in your class. She likes to hang around you. She is so blessed with sensitivity that she stands by others who need compassion or loyalty. She will sacrifice personal freedom to be a close friend. She has no ulterior motives that you can detect. You think Ruth will make a great wife for someone someday—if she ever can stretch the ties that bind her faithfulness to others.

What can you learn from Ruth? The standard answer involves some act of loyalty you could have—should have—for those who need you. Ruth as a role model is among the best, worthy of application and teaching to your students. But perhaps there is more.

First, Ruth provides an important case in God's history of salvation, as He tells it in His Word. She didn't know her future, but God did. He had grand plans! She gave birth to a son, Obed. Obed became the grandfather of King David. And you know who else was in that ancient family's future? Jesus Himself! Ruth eventually appeared in the genealogy of the Savior—by name—in Matthew 1. She is a vital and most blessed historical link between Jesus and His ancestors.

Second, Ruth's faithfulness reminds us of God's faithfulness. Do you sometimes wrestle to get away from your Savior, only to realize that He will not let go? Oh, your wrestling may not reek of rebelliousness, but it does smell of sin. You and many modern Christians still pull away toward favorite sins. Or maybe it's a brief excursion to sample temptations that appear especially delightful. But Jesus holds on, telling you how much He loves you, and never restraining you from other choices. Yes, if you really want to leave Him, you can go. Others can't take you, but you can go of your own accord.

Third, God loves and calls women to serve Him. Sometimes their service is mighty and spectacular, and sometimes it is more common, without a lot of notice—except by God. Deborah was authoritative and militant, Rebekah was clever and bold to take risks, and Ruth was sacrificially loving and compassionate. All were God's servants; all were saints and sinners. The Holy Spirit worked in and through them to bless future generations.

You and the staff that serve your school are no less servants and tools of the Holy Spirit than other servants revealed in the Bible. Man or woman, student or parent—all have God's mission before them: to proclaim the Gospel so others may be saved from their sins and praise God.

Next time you feel a child tugging on your slacks or tapping you on your shoulder, think of Ruth. Think of Jesus. Think of yourself too. Don't let go of those kids!

❖ **Background Reading:**
Ruth 1:1–18

31

Luke

· · · · · · · · · · · · · · ·

Inasmuch as many have undertaken to compile a narrative of the things that have been accomplished among us, just as those who from the beginning were eyewitnesses and ministers of the word have delivered them to us, it seemed good to me also, having followed all things closely for some time past, to write an orderly account for you, most excellent Theophilus, that you may have certainty concerning the things you have been taught. (Luke 1:1–4)

· · · · · · · · · · · · · · ·

Imagine that Luke is in your class. He is your best science student. Though enamored with science, he also possesses aptitude for organization, writing, people skills, and adventure. As editor of the school newspaper, he reported minute details of young Tara's cut and scrapes after falling from the swing. His report is accurate, because he was with Tara right after she fell, attempting to comfort her and administer first aid. With all his gifts, you pray for his success in the scientific community—and think he would make a good minister too.

If you weren't a teacher, what else would you—could you—do?

While the Holy Spirit led you to teach in a Christian school, it isn't the only vocation or ministry that offered career potential. Effective educators also possess penchants for a variety of avocational or extra-vocational skills and knowledge.

What "extras" do you bring to your classroom? Don't be modest now. Or haven't you thought about it? God blessed you with a variety of gifts. Among you and other staff members, you probably could put together an impressive extra-curricular program! And what would make such an effort spectacular is that you would demonstrate that Christian vocation involves all God-pleasing work and pastimes.

What is it that transforms human-centered jobs and hobbies into Christ-centered vocation? The devil, who often acts as a career counselor, would have us believe that a person's effort, performance, and demeanor are what separate Christian life from life independent of Christ. This scheme threatens Christians, even devout ones who want to please God on their own—and forget their inability or disability to do so.

Christian vocation affects how one approaches and executes tasks. God blesses the approach and execution because of Jesus' approach to and execution of His task of taking away the sins of the world. That accomplished, God sent the Holy Spirit to permeate all of life. A significant portion of that life still suffers from sin's effects.

You have observed that Christian vocation and non-Christian vocation can appear shockingly similar in practitioners. Unbelievers have contributed generously to the welfare of humanity, sometimes appearing more Christian than Christians! Yep, that's the devil at work again, taunting, "So what's so great about being a Christian? You Christians have vocations built upon hypocrisy!"

The devil is so after you! He taunts, "Aside from a cross on the wall [You do have one, don't you?], what makes your classroom so special? How does your vocation differ from your counterpart in the public school?"

Your only true defense is to claim your special condition as forgiven sinner. This is the asset you bring to your vocation. And more—your motivation for all you do springs from all that Christ has done for you.

Learning from Luke, we see a physician transformed into a minister by the Holy Spirit working through the Word. Luke became Paul's companion, an international traveler whose primary role was to proclaim and teach the Gospel. And you can be certain that he never abandoned his other skills as he served people.

Luke and you have a lot in common.

❖ **Background Reading:**
Acts 1:1–3

32

Moses

· · · · · · · · · · · · · · ·

But he said, "Oh, my Lord, please send someone else." Then the anger of the LORD was kindled against Moses and He said, "Is there not Aaron, your brother, the Levite? I know that he can speak well. Behold, he is coming out to meet you, and when he sees you, he will be glad in his heart. You shall speak to him and put the words in his mouth, and I will be with your mouth and with his mouth and will teach you both what to do." (Exodus 4:13–15)

· · · · · · · · · · · · · · ·

Imagine that Moses is in your class. He gets poor grades on class participation. When coerced, he grudgingly participates, and he does it well. Moses came to you with an international background, and he was adopted by a wealthy family. He is a bit volatile; you might refer him for anger management. He often feels sorry for himself when things don't go exactly as he plans.

Projecting Moses into your class might be frightening. He is known for his plagues on an uncooperative Pharaoh; just think what might happen to the drinking fountain (a.k.a. bubbler) or the playground if you refused any of his propositions! Hmm. But that's not what God would want us to learn from Moses' life and his service to God's people.

Teaching requires confidence in speaking to groups. Some teachers are confident before any group; others might experience anxiety before preschoolers or middle schoolers. High school could be terrifying to a teacher allergic to rolling eyeballs or other manifestations of the dreaded *ho-hums*. You may be comfortable in front of a bustling classroom but quake in front of peers. Moses suggests a solution for public presentations that unnerve you: Whine. And not the grape kind, either!

God heard Moses' complaints, but He wouldn't release him from a task that would crumble and cripple most church workers. Instead, God provided for Moses' weakness by furnishing a helper— kind of like a classroom aide!

You know that teaching is difficult and demanding. You also know that you don't perform as well on some aspects of teaching as you do on others. Sin—your own as well as that of others—prevents perfection. You may find aspects of Christian pedagogy so difficult that you're tempted to labor for Jesus in some other vocation. You might even whine.

How will God help you confront your Moses Moments? It's doubtful that a multi-talented aide will suddenly appear in your classroom tomorrow morning, having strengths where you have weaknesses. In some (many?) cases, God wants us to be the answer to our prayers. Turn whine into prayer for a good first step.

Talk to God about your weaknesses and fears. He may not do what you hope for, but He will not be angry if you ask. Tell God that you want to serve in His name despite your flaws. Ask Him to send His Holy Spirit to guide you. Of course, you must accept the Spirit's guidance, which may be radically different from what you expect. And how will you know the Spirit's direction? Not to suggest limitations on the Spirit's methods, but the most reliable way known is through God's existing Word.

The same God who sent Jesus to take away your sins will provide other good news in His Word. Find time to sit back and read. And keep your whine glass empty.

❖ **Background Reading:**
Exodus 4:1–30

33

Mordecai

· · · · · · · · · · · · · · · ·

Then Mordecai told them to reply to Esther,
"Do not think to yourself that in the king's
palace you will escape any more than all the
other Jews. For if you keep silent at this time,
relief and deliverance will rise for the Jews from
another place, but you and your father's house
will perish. And who knows whether you have
not come to the kingdom for such a time as
this?" (Esther 4:13–14)

· · · · · · · · · · · · · · · ·

Imagine that Mordecai is in your class. You
think he might grow up to be a public defender.
For now, he knows every rule in the school hand-
book. He is not above telling an errant teacher
when a supposed rule really is only supposed—a
figment of the teacher's wishful thinking. Mordecai also applies the rules to himself. Mostly,
Mordecai likes to avoid legalistic confrontations
by acting before defense or prosecution of classmates or teachers are necessary. He is a propo-

nent of fair treatment and an advocate for the underdog.

Your role may be similar to that of Mordecai's. By himself, Mordecai had no power. His asset was listening. He listened in on conversations around him. Since he wasn't boisterous or intrusive, people felt free to talk around him, as if he weren't there. That's how Mordecai uncovered a plot to kill the king and thus prevented a tragedy.

God made Mordecai a good listener, just as He Himself is a good listener. God hears the problems of His people and Satan's plots against them. God acts to protect His people. He heard His helpless people's cries for salvation, and He sent Jesus to rescue them. He still hears us. He still rescues us. Because we are so blessed, He expects us to bless others.

Teachers need to put on their Mordecai ears. As God's servants, they need to listen to students. Yes, this involves eavesdropping whenever it seems appropriate for the safety of students. You need to hear their fears, their plans, and their needs—including the need for discipline, repentance, mercy, and forgiveness.

Today's classrooms always are at risk. Satan has an arsenal of weapons to attack God's people. You must guard against outsiders and insiders alike. Like Mordecai, you can't always address problems yourself. You may have to call on administrators, pastors, or community resources. Most of all, you need to call on God. It's no coincidence that you are where you are when you are.

The greatest threat to your students involves the battle for their souls. Satan would be tickled red to spiritually slaughter you and your students. But Satan most often is an insidious and subtle spiritual virus. Satan likes to work right where you wouldn't expect him. Though his ears must burn every time he hears "Jesus Loves Me, This I Know" or "Amazing Grace," he knows success lies in deception and surprise.

Listen for Satan. You will hear his influence if you are in the right place. Pray that the Spirit moves you there, opens your ears to hear God's Word, gives you godly judgment, and gives you courage to act. Perhaps you'll be the next one present for "such a time as this."

❖ **Background Reading:**

Esther 10

34

Mark
(a.k.a. John Mark)

. . . .

*And there arose a sharp disagreement,
so that they [Paul and John Mark] separated
from each other. Barnabas took Mark with
him and sailed away to Cyprus, but Paul
chose Silas and departed, having been
commended by the brothers to the grace
of the Lord. (Acts 15:39–40)*

. . . .
. . . .

*Luke alone is with me [Paul]. Get Mark and
bring him with you, for he is very useful to me
for ministry. (2 Timothy 4:11)*

. . . .

Imagine that Mark—often called John Mark—is
in your class. He would prefer homeschooling to
your classroom. Sometimes, John Mark asks to
go home in the middle of the day, because he is

sick. Homesick, more than likely. You find it easy to be angry at John Mark because you can't rely on his presence when you teach a new concept. But, as a professional educator—and a warm human being—you always find a way to welcome him when he returns to school.

You sometimes act like John Mark. You would rather be home than supervising after-school care, figuring out how to work the interactive whiteboard, meeting the parents who think you're the worst teacher in the world, or cleaning up the results of a sudden epidemic of stomach flu. Who could blame you if you walked off the job? The list is short but in control of your future employment.

Other situations are more crucial. Perhaps you would rather be home than confronting problems with faith. Will you ever get through to the parent of another denomination who is livid with you after his son paid close attention (just like him to listen carefully *for the first time*!) to your teaching about infant Baptism? And if only you could skip a response to the parent who wants to let her child wait until she is older to decide about faith. (The child definitely will decide!) The classic, of course, is the parent who will never allow the dirty word *sin* to be applied to *his* child. Who could blame you if you walked off the job? This list is even shorter! Don't expect a sympathetic exemption from God.

Spiritual hostility isn't the only challenge that you would prefer to avoid. Spiritual depression and despondency impose powerful effects on teachers who labor to instruct and inspire children in the faith. Have you students who just don't believe what Jesus did for them? Are these the same students who hunt for spiritual rest but can't accept the truth that would comfort them? It's enough to depress you! Who would blame you if you just let it go by with an "it is what it is" attitude?

You wouldn't be alone if you've found yourself in a John Mark situation. But there is a remedy. You know it as repentance and forgiveness. Jesus gave His life to make this remedy possible. John Mark had it—from God and from Paul, whom he had let down. John Mark kept working for Jesus, even after he abandoned Paul. He just found a different team—an alternative you might consider yourself instead of just leaving the education ministry, if that is on your heart. Or it might be that spiritual growth will rectify the situation.

Whatever you do, don't give up. You are useful for ministry!

❖ **Background Reading:**
Acts 15:36–41

35

Lazarus

. . . .

Six days before the Passover, Jesus therefore came to Bethany, where Lazarus was, whom Jesus had raised from the dead. (John 12:1)

. . . .

Imagine that Lazarus is in your class. People would consider Lazarus a medical miracle because both his breathing and his heart stopped. The EMTs did everything they could—and it worked! Most of his classmates praise God for his recovery, but a few kids think that Lazarus gets too much attention. He is this year's school and community celebrity.

Life-and-death-and-life stories garner national headlines. Many of those situations are unexplainable; therefore, they are mysteriously cast as miracles—and everyone celebrates. God rarely gets the credit.

How many students in your classroom believe that Jesus is their Savior? Not that you want a bunch of nosy reporters probing your school, but that number is how many life-and-death-and-life stories sit right in your classroom. Praise God! He has brought them from death to life.

The same is true for you. You have gone from death to life. (By the end of the school year, you might even look that way!) Who gets the credit? The triune God, of course. Father, Son, and Holy Spirit make the process possible.

God the Father started the process. It remains a mysterious miracle how He knew you even as He created dinosaurs and roses and broccoli. He had plans for you—to take away your sins and provide life for you even after you die. Your life is a miracle. And whatever thoughts you have as you glance over your class each day, praise God that students too are miracles.

Jesus Christ, God's own Son, made the miracle possible through His life, death, and resurrection. Because He lives, we too shall live. That biblical message has been proclaimed for centuries. The apostle Paul said that had Jesus not risen from the dead, faith would be in vain. Look at your class again. Look at yourself in a mirror too. Your sins are among the trillions that nailed Jesus to the cross, and He paid for each one of them. More than that, He took all of them away to make you righteous before God. And even more, He is the power that will bring you back to life after you die!

The Holy Spirit brings the gift of salvation and faith to you and your students. Not everyone believes or knows Jesus as their Savior. You do. Ask your kids. Many do too. You believe the impossible because the Holy Spirit opened your soul, body, and mind to the truth. You call it faith and trust. Faith is like a pair of eyeglasses or contacts that allow you to see what unbelievers cannot. For example, when is the last time you looked at a Bible and considered it a mere book? Or when is the last time you saw a baby baptized and considered it just a quaint tradition? Most important, when is the last time you saw an artist's depiction of Jesus and thought of Him as just a good guy from long ago?

You have the miracle of faith. You once were dead. God brought you to life. It will happen again.

❖ **Background Reading:**
John 11:1–43

36

Barnabas

· · · · · · · · · · · · · · · ·

The report of this came to the ears of the church in Jerusalem, and they sent Barnabas to Antioch. When he came and saw the grace of God, he was glad, and he exhorted them all to remain faithful to the Lord with steadfast purpose, for he was a good man, full of the Holy Spirit and of faith. And a great many people were added to the Lord. (Acts 11:22–24)

· · · · · · · · · · · · · · · ·

Imagine that Barnabas is in your class. You could use a few more boys like him. You wouldn't hear put-downs or negative talk. Barnabas is the one whose behavior actually matches his name, which means *encourager*. (You've had a child named *Angel* in one of your classes, haven't you?) Barnabas is the one to help a struggling math student or befriend the *Eeyore* in your class. Admit it; he is your favorite recess conversationalist too!

Your students benefit more from encouragement than from praise. Praise, rightly applied, is dispensed to the successful student, regardless of effort applied. Some students expect praise just for existing, and too many parents support that position. So praise, lavishly supplied, might go like this: "Your math paper was so sloppy that I couldn't mark anything wrong. Good job!" Or maybe it springs to life this way: "You are a sinner; that surely gives you lots to repent about. Great!"

Sin, both original and personal, normally sobers life. How can you praise what isn't praise-worthy? How can you feel good about performing poorly? How painful is reality? Praise in any of those situations will be hollow or deceptive. You and your students need a Barnabas intervention!

You know people who are upbeat all the time. You probably wonder what is wrong with them—whether they know what's going on around them. Had you observed Barnabas, you might have thought the same of him. But Barnabas's encouragement didn't originate in him. His was godly encouragement—and more than just words. When John Mark was expelled from Paul's trip, Barnabas took John Mark on an alternate missionary effort. Presumably, John Mark matured and later became one of Paul's "pets."

Your ministry as a teacher requires you to encourage students. Chances are good that they need lots of encouragement. The newer believers in your class may especially need encouragement. They need reminders of God's unconditional love, His welcoming of repeated repentance, and His endless supply of forgiveness. They need encouragement to worship and to learn more about their Savior, Jesus. They need help living their faith as both saint and sinner. Since you have lots of experience in these areas, you are the perfect—okay, not-quite-perfect—encourager for them.

Like Barnabas, your well of encouragement is rooted in your relationship with Jesus. He never gives up on you but cheers you ahead with rich and plentiful applications of the Gospel. Thanking God for that blessing will fuel your encouragement for others.

> ❖ **Background Reading:**
> **Acts 9–15**

37

Martha

· · · · · · · · · · · · · · · ·

But Martha was distracted with much serving.
(Luke 10:40a)

· · · · · · · · · · · · · · · ·

Imagine that Martha is in your class. She is the one wiping down the whiteboard, booting the classroom computers, arranging the positions of the desks, and helping you raise your standards of tidiness. Martha is reliable. She will do what you ask, and then add some value to it. She will also cry if you give classroom jobs to others or if you downplay the need for her level of organization. Martha complains about other students not helping, but she does so much herself that there is piddling need for others.

How would you measure up against Martha? Now there is a double-edged question! You might busy yourself with necessary tasks, as she did, and that would seem good to some and bad to others. Yes, chairs need to be set up for parent meetings, coffee made for the faculty, desks sanitized in the war against the spread of the flu virus, ventilation adjusted in each room, and kitchen readied for the looming threat of a health department visit. And that's only the beginning.

You might have a different perspective on priorities, and that would seem good to some and bad to others. Taking ten minutes behind closed doors for daily meditation on God's Word is more important than meeting other more tangible daily demands. Let the Good News of Jesus' sacrifice and love for you bless, strengthen, and motivate you. Praying for students, each by name, preempts a clean whiteboard or satisfying the morning coffee fix. Seeking the Spirit's guidance in dealing with anticipated problems takes precedent over assuring a full tissue box on your desk.

Perspective is a gift. Every school needs a dependable work master. The expanded truth is that every school needs more than one to relieve the work maniac from the intimidating to-do list. Finding the median between workaholic and apathetic is a gift. And, for the Christian teacher, it is requisite for God-pleasing service to congregation, school, students, parents, and colleagues. Okay, so therein lies the rub, as Shakespeare might say if he taught seventh grade in your school. You serve many people.

Jesus would understand that dilemma. How many times didn't crowds drive Him to exhaustion? He simply could not escape the multitudes pleading for healing and begging His blessing. He couldn't retreat far from His detractors either—kind of like you in the grocery story or church pew. To serve or not to serve, that is the question.

Jesus' comment to Martha is the focal point in addressing the question of service. The remedy lies in balance. The remediation lies in the eager "yes" and the humble but unapologetic "no."

Remember, you have a primary ministry to perform, and you must have energy to accomplish it. By virtue of your Spirit-filled empowerment, you must attend first to growing in faith and proclaiming the Gospel. And you must take care never to give the impression that menial tasks are below your dignity or status. (Remembering how Jesus washed His disciples' feet will help maintain that perspective.)

You are a servant. You are a leader—at least in your classroom. Serve well and lead well, with the help of God.

By the way, are you sure you made enough snacks for the gathering at which this devotion is to be read?

❖ **Background Reading:**
Luke 10:38–42

38

Job

. . . .

For I know that my Redeemer lives, and at the last He will stand upon the earth. And after my skin has been thus destroyed, yet in my flesh I shall see God, whom I shall see for myself, and my eyes shall behold, and not another. My heart faints within me! (Job 19:25–27)

. . . .

Imagine that Job is in your class. Students refuse to sit next to Job because he is accident-prone. He would be the one walking home under fair blue skies only to have a small black cloud dash in and drench him. Or if there are a few stray *E. coli* in the school lunch, they will lodge in Job. Or if you misplace a note about taking medicine at 2:00 p.m. (to combat the *E. coli*), it will be his. Yet Job seems blessed with higher levels of endurance and quiet trust that life will get better, and if it doesn't, well, at the very least (which actually is the very most), Job knows that Jesus lives and he will too.

You do your share of suffering, not that much of it compares to Job's episodes. But personal suffering is specific rather than relative to others. Bucking up to teach through a severe cold because your school's budget is short on substitute pay feels like sacrificial suffering, acute with momentary and real misery. Coping with small paychecks or wondering if you'll ever retire threatens your trust in God's care. Oh, you know He will take care of you, but you really hope for comfort and convenience. And you are uneasy about your family too. What will happen when violent weather roars through their city? And how you pray that the cars of drunk drivers stay far away from that of your loved ones during their long drive to visit you!

You know that Job's story of faith is supposed to increase your trust—make your faith in God's care stronger. But if you sneak a long peek at all of Job's story, you see real life. You see conflict with doubts, advice from friends, and even a little anger at God for permitting a good life to turn foul.

You know that your Redeemer lives, and it isn't just because Job told you or that it's a popular hymn to sing on Easter or at funerals. Your entire life is wrapped around Jesus and what He did to your sins and suffering—what He did on the cross and in the tomb. Talk about suffering! Jesus knows even more than Job.

Have you watched any students suffer? Divorce exacts its price, and abuse inflicts its dark consequences. Accidents and disease send students and faculty scurrying off to pray. Chronic conflict warps relationships with parents and colleagues. Suffering, sin's number one liability and Satan's staple, attempts to shroud Jesus' message of hope, healing, and heaven.

Looking for good news in all of this? First, you are still here. Suffering may slow you down a bit, but it hasn't destroyed you or the service you perform in the name of Jesus. Second, by the power of the Holy Spirit working through Word and sacrament, you will persist and persevere. And most important . . .

. . . you know that your Redeemer lives!

❖ **Background Reading:**
Job 1:1–12

39

Delilah

. . . .

And she [Delilah] said to him [Samson], "How can you say, 'I love you,' when your heart is not with me? You have mocked me these three times, and you have not told me where your great strength lies." And when she pressed him hard with her words day after day, and urged him, his soul was vexed to death. (Judges 16:15–16)

. . . .

Imagine that Delilah is in your class. You can't miss her. Neither can anyone else. Her skirt rises or falls depending on who is watching. The rest of her wardrobe leaves little to the imagination and much to be desired—by the adolescent males. Delilah can even sluttify school uniforms. [Don't look it up; it's a new word invented just for Delilah.] Female classmates are jealous of Delilah's success with the boys. In fact, she is teaching them that manipulating male willpower is uncomplicated if one uses lots of makeup and dirty talk.

Classroom Delilahs hinder learning while ruining their reputations. They are a common annoyance and hindrance in Christian schools. Attempts to control their attention-getting behavior may meet with letter-of-the-law rules governing decency, but such rules often defeat themselves with myriad loopholes. Besides, life within the classroom occupies only a short portion of students' days and an even shorter portion of their lives. All this may lead you to question why Delilahs are allowed in Christian schools.

What good are they? What can we possibly do for them? The answer is an emphatic "Who knows?"

But, think about it: you might make a case for asking those questions about *all* of your students, even though their sinfulness may be less . . . uh . . . noticeable. Yet, we can judge only on the surface, and that doesn't always work well. (Consider this: Samson, who fell to Delilah's charms, was a judge!) If you're a veteran teacher, you know of several delightful students who ended up doing awful things. Okay, Christian classrooms would be more pleasant places if teachers didn't have to deal with Delilahs and assorted delinquents, but still . . .

Maybe God sent them to you. Consider how the Master Teacher operated.

He targeted the more obvious sinners, including the Delilah and delinquent types. He didn't let what He saw affect His compassion and strategy to address their real needs. Others who were more outwardly devout thought it scandalous that Jesus was so friendly with sinners. By the time He was done with them, they were forgiven sinners. In the end (or the beginning, depending on how you look at it), He would die for them—come alive for them—and live with them forever.

God sent sinners to your classroom. You'll not see the results of your teaching and witnessing for some of them, because some will not change. Others will look the same, but their hearts will have been influenced by you, and they really love Jesus and like you. Inward transformation can take time to break through hardened exteriors. But God may bestow on you a few students who change before your eyes. (When is the last time one of your students was baptized? It happens more than 2,000 times each year in Lutheran schools!)

Yes, God definitely sent Delilahs and delinquents to your classroom. So don't blame the principal.

❖ **Background Reading:**
Judges 16:4–19

40

Jesus

· · · · · · · · · · · · · · · ·

He is not here, for He has risen, as He said.
(Matthew 28:6)

· · · · · · · · · · · · · · · ·

Imagine that Jesus is in your class. His eyes smile as much as His lips. Other students like to be in His company because He always is kind and considerate. Leadership comes naturally to Jesus, but so does serving others. It's hard to believe that any student could be as good as Jesus. Sometimes you wish He would "act up" a little, but that happens only when someone mocks His Father or attacks His brothers or sisters. Jesus is truly one of a kind.

You don't need imagination.

Jesus is in your classroom. What do you suppose would happen if you and your students suddenly could see Him? Would you rivet your attention on all the details in your lesson plan? (You do have a lesson plan, right?) Would you strain to use just the right words and to lovingly interact with your students?

What do you think would happen if your students suddenly saw Jesus? Now that's something you would like to witness, right? Winsome behavior! Students treating you and their classmates with warm respect. Think of the improvement in homework, both in quality and in completion rate. Family dogs would go hungry as assignments disappeared from their diet.

Would Jesus' power to transform lives transform your classroom? Probably not. At least not for long.

Jesus is perfect, but His followers aren't. (Yet.) His presence, suddenly seen, would likely result in fear—the kind assumed in those "fear, love, and trust" statements in the catechism. Nothing reveals sin so clearly as the thought of an all-knowing, all-seeing, all-powerful God. In addition, sadly, some parents equate Christian schools and congregations to places where students and adults always behave as if they knew God was standing nearby, sort of on divine supervision.

Knowledge of personal sin as well as original sin is only one part of Christian education. Teachers who listen to what Jesus teaches know better—the *better* being what Jesus did about their sins.

Your class will never be sinless. But your class always can be forgiven. Jesus Himself didn't bother with perfecting the behavior of others. Forgiving sins to change lives forever was more His speed. Transformed human lives involved hating sin and loving others as He did—as much as humanly possible. Grace and mercy, in the name of Jesus, is the hallmark of Christian classrooms.

So what do your students see when they look at you? Do they shrink in terror? Snicker in disrespect? Or warm themselves in the glow of your love?

Thank God for what you have learned from Jesus. You already know the most important thing you could ever know. And there is more. Someday you will experience the perfect life for which you have long yearned.

Invite your students to come along. They, too, have learned from Jesus. And won't that be the field trip to end all field trips!

❖ **Background Reading:**
   Book of Matthew